dog
parties

dog
parties

entertaining your party animals

Gibbs Smith, Publisher
Salt Lake City

KIMBERLY SCHLEGEL WHITMAN
WITH COURTNEY DRESLIN
PHOTOGRAPHY BY STEPHEN KARLISCH

First Edition

10 09 08 07 06   5 4 3 2 1

Published by

Gibbs Smith, Publisher

P.O. Box 667

Layton, Utah 84041

Orders: 1.800.748.5439

www.gibbs-smith.com

Designed by m:GraphicDesign / Maralee Oleson

Printed and bound in Hong Kong

Library of Congress Control Number: 2006925126

ISBN 1-4236-0087-8

TO MY GRAMMA SCHLEGEL, FROM WHOM I
"INHERITED" MY PASSION FOR PETS AND WHO
SHARED LOLA'S BIRTHDAY; AND TO AXEL, A
FAITHFUL AND TRUE MEMBER OF OUR FAMILY
FOR SO LONG. I MISS YOU BOTH . . .

contents

a concise history of pooch pampering

SOMEONE A LONG TIME AGO GOT IT RIGHT WHEN THEY TERMED DOGS "MAN'S BEST FRIEND." THERE IS NO DOUBT THAT DOGS BRING JOY TO MANY, MANY LIVES. DURING CHILDHOOD, THEY ARE OUR PLAYMATES. AS WE GROW OLDER, THEY BECOME OUR SURROGATE CHILDREN. IN LATER YEARS, THEY EASE THE TRANSITION INTO AN EMPTY NEST AND REPLACE THE COMPANIONSHIP OF DEPARTED SPOUSES. DOGS COMFORT THE LONELY, HELP TO HEAL THE SICK, AND LIFT SPIRITS WHEREVER THEY GO. THERE IS SIMPLY NO BETTER EXAMPLE OF LOYALTY AND LOVE THAN THAT OF A DOG.

The love affair with dogs is visible everywhere these days, from luxury-brand dog carriers, collars, and clothing to dog specialty spas, fitness centers, and camps. Some airlines even offer frequent flier miles for dogs who jet-set along with their owners. But this is not a mere pop culture trend. From the earliest of times, humans on all corners of the globe have been showing off their love of *le chien*. When I wanted to learn more about pampered pooches in history, I turned to my dear friend Summerlee Staten, "mother" to Beaufort the Pekingese and the best researcher I know. Here is what she found:

• Domesticated dogs were honored members of society in ancient Egypt and their birth was celebrated second only to that of a son. The pharaohs kept their dogs in elaborate kennels and assigned personal handlers to attend them. Egyptian tombs were often decorated with images of their dogs, and many pet dogs were even mummified and buried with their owners.

• As early as 2000 b.c., the Pekingese breed was worshipped in the temples of China. These dogs were carried in ornate jade doghouses and attended all imperial celebrations, where they feasted on luxurious foods and teas. Small Pekes, called "sleeves," were held in the folds of their ladies' robes. They were bestowed with royal titles and were designated as heads of state. It was also customary for the emperor to choose four Pekes to serves as his bodyguards. These four Pekes would precede the emperor at royal gatherings, holding the hem of his royal robe in their mouths.

• In the 1800s, England's Queen Victoria was presented with a Pekingese called Looty, who had been stolen from the Forbidden City during a British raid. The Pekingese went on to become a favorite breed of aristocrats in London and were often paraded around in hats and elaborate costumes. At least one Pekingese was knighted in a special ceremony.

• In Tibet, Lhasa Apso dogs were nurtured by the dalai lamas and were considered holy. They were placed on bright silk pillows in a place of honor at religious ceremonies and were believed to bring protection to all attending. They were often given as gifts and were believed to bless the recipient with good fortune.

• During the Middle Ages and the Renaissance, elegant women began to carry their small dogs with them everywhere. Specialized groomers, called "demoiselles," were responsible for making dogs presentable to "go out"—bathing them and then trimming and styling their hair to mimic the popular hairstyles of the day.

• This fascination with dogs was not a phenomena limited to women. Men fell under their spell as well. King Henry III of France coddled his miniature Bichon Frises in tiny baskets worn around his neck, and his dogs were famously pampered, perfumed, and decorated with ribbons. This led to the French word *bichonner*, which means "to pamper."

• In twentieth-century India, the Maharaja of Junagadh had more than 800 dogs. Each resided in a personal room and was attended to by a personal servant. Dogs were invited to parties and allowed to travel—with engraved silver bowls and silk travel coats. The Maharaja even held a spectacular wedding for his Bull Terrier, Roshanara. The bride was dipped in perfume and dressed in brocade and diamonds. She was carried on a silver palanquin to her groom, Bobby, a Golden Retriever, who was decked out in gold bracelets and necklaces. Hundreds of guests and 250 dogs dressed in brocade attended the grand feast and three-day-long celebration.

• The Duke and Duchess of Windsor were renowned for spoiling their Pugs, whom they considered substitute children. They ate off of silver trays and were followed around by professional "poop scoopers." The Windsors also employed a "doggie chef" to make sure the pooches' meals were varied. In 1998, Sotheby's auctioned off some of the couple's antiques (including some Pug-related items) and threw a "Pug Reception and Tea" to honor the Windsors' love of the breed. More than 110 Pugs enjoyed dog biscuits passed by strolling attendants as their owners sipped champagne and tea.

• Even American presidents have gotten in on the act. From George Washington's Foxhounds to George W. Bush's Scottie, First Dogs make the White House a cozier home for the First Family. Fala, Franklin Roosevelt's beloved Scottish Terrier, was photographed at many historic events, including the Atlantic Charter Conferences with Sir Winston Churchill and the Quebec Conferences. Roosevelt made sure that a bone was brought up for Fala each morning on the president's breakfast tray. Barney, the current First Scot, has a birthday party in September, where he has worn a birthday cone hat and feasted on a cookie cake made especially for him. He and Miss Beazley, the newest Presidential Scottie, have even been known to give their own press conferences.

Of course, you need not be a celebrity or diplomat to pamper your pet. A few years ago, I decided to celebrate the unique bond between humans and dogs with a garden party for my Chihuahua, Lola, and her friends. This event brought so much happiness to both the dogs and their owners that we decided to make dog parties a regular part of our lives. With this book, I hope you find party ideas and inspirations for spreading the love and licks and feel confident to create your own special thank-you to that treasured four-legged companion. The bond between humans and dogs is truly something to celebrate!

Kimberly Schlegel Whitman

BY BETTY LOU PHILLIPS, GUEST WRITER

s-paw party

ROMANS MAY HAVE DISCOVERED THE SPA, BUT NOT TO BE OUTDONE, AMERICANS HAVE BROUGHT WHAT WAS ONCE A LUXURY RESERVED FOR THE PRIVILEGED INTO THE TWENTY-FIRST CENTURY.

Until a few years ago, health resorts were spots where we enjoyed massages and herbal body wraps. And now? Bowing to our society's passion for its pets, more than a handful of spas have gone to the dogs—literally.

No matter that originally to spa was "to bathe"—flowing from the Latin *salus per aqua*, meaning "health through water." Or that showering affection on our animal companions traditionally meant a flea bath before a play date at a nearby dog park. In a country where stress knows no age, much less class, to spa has taken on an entirely new meaning without loosing its cachet. Indeed, treating the pooch to a day of beauty is the preferred way to express devotion.

So, guests were prompt on the balmy morning when Jackson, a one-year-old Norwich terrier, had invited twenty-five canines to gather in his backyard. With all the makings of a full-service resort—including the gurgling fountain—he aimed to help friends who had names like Britney, Max, Oscar, and Harry prepare for an haute summer, which in Dallas, Texas, can be terribly hot.

And like at the posh Canyon Ranch, Greenhouse, and Golden Door spas, the treatment was nothing short of royal. There were terry robes for tail-wagging spa-goers to walk around in, paw readers and pet therapists to consult between massages and pet-icures with paw-lish.

Here are the niceties that made for a day as special as those who milled about.

15

THE INVITATION: COME. SIT. STAY.

Befitting a party mood, those invited were asked to appear fashionably fetching, of course. Also, they were specifically requested to put their best foot forward, avoiding any faux-paws such as barking, digging up the host's exquisitely manicured yard, or getting in scrapes, which might put a damper on the day. Leaving nothing to chance, cushioned chaises set up poolside offered wide-angle views, making it easy for faithful companions to keep a watchful eye on their charges and discourage any rowdiness.

BOWTIQUE

A one-stop shop offered grooming products as well as ready-to-wear for four-legged fashion victims to add to their already packed closets. Among the tempting accessories were chic sunglasses, collars, bedding, perfume, and toys.

THE CHECK-IN

Heralding a day that promised lots of fun, 100 purple and green helium-filled balloons floated in the air as Jackson enthusiastically welcomed Bailey and Annie. Meanwhile, the team of specialists checked for Ashton's, Sam's, Riese's, and Rusty's names on the list.

TABLE SETTINGS
Custom-colored lavender cloths coated fittingly with paw prints made clear there would be no eating from a bowl off the floor. Smart slipcovered cushions begged everyone to "Sit." On accompanying chair backs? "Bone Appétit." Napkins were lawn green, naturally. And the centerpieces— sterling silver dog bowls filled with grass— became conversation pieces, not surprisingly.

PHOTO OPS

Not everyone wanted to be photographed in their swimsuits, which was understandable. But most were not the least bit camera-shy when it came to family portraits.

MUSIC

"Roll Over Beethoven," "Tails of the City," and "Pet Melodies" drifted across the grounds.

BONE APPÉTIT

Waiters with silver trays offered an appetizing array of all-natural bite-size treats. Cool bottled water imported from distant places was the favored "Pooch Punch" and encouraged honored guests to revel in the day's splendor. Meanwhile, best friends chatted over curried chicken tea sandwiches and those of radish and cucumber. Fresh fruit skewers, too, were courtesy of The Food Company. Then there was Pacuiggo Italian ice and Jamba Juice smoothies or iced tea brewed with fresh herbs.

HONORED SPEAKER

Dallasite Allison Merrill, D.M.V., presented valuable tips on how to develop cooperative relationships, plus insight on keeping pets healthy.

SERVICES AVAILABLE AT GROOMING STATIONS

Blow-drys, massages, and pet-icures with a choice of Opi sparkling pink, green, or lavender nail "pawlish" were among the services available to those willing to work at keeping up appearances.

"DOGGIE" BAGS

A babble ball, oatmeal shampoo and conditioner, and towel begging pets to wipe their paws were going-away gifts. But "Paw Prints"—a photo album of the day's festivities—was the best present of all, ensuring that the day would long be remembered.

lola's birthday party

IN HONOR OF LOLA THE CHIHUAHUA'S THIRD BIRTHDAY (THAT'S 21 IN DOG YEARS), FORTY OF HER MOST STYLISH POOCH PALS WERE INVITED TO PUT THEIR BEST PAWS FORWARD AT A SUNDAY-AFTERNOON SOIREE.

To ensure that the guests would have plenty of room to frolic, the party was held in the vast gardens of Lola's grandparents' home, a venue that is the yard of every dog's dreams, even without the super-sized bones scattered around the manicured lawn for this gathering. Since this space is enclosed, leashes are optional.

In lieu of a traditional guest book, guests signed autograph dogs from Legacy Trading Company.

DOG FOOD AND PEOPLE FOOD

Refreshments for the dogs looked every bit as appetizing as those for the owners. So, to avoid confusion, strolling attendants passed the human snacks, while treats for the dogs were displayed on tables. The people food included Chihuahua cheese quesadillas, smoked turkey salad sandwiches in the shape of bones, and hot dogs with puff pastries on each end.

The doggie buffet table held an elaborate assortment of real dog bones, canine cupcakes, and sugar cookies—all displayed in pink glass containers surrounded by flowers, a setup that allowed owners to choose specific treats for their four-legged companions (although a few of the larger dogs served themselves). Water coolers on "dog level" were also adorned with flowers and assured that Lola's friends would stay refreshed.

FESTIVITIES AND FAVORS

Special activities for the guests of honor included their very own caricature sketches and massages by doggie masseuses on loan from a dog spa and fitness center. The latter indulgence didn't go over quite so well with some breeds; for instance, Gabby, a Yorkshire terrier, hopped off the massage cot and tried to make a run for it. It seems that doggie massages are more successful at the spa's private rooms where the dogs aren't distracted by their parents looking on and friends frolicking nearby. All the while, plenty of pooches splashed about in the fountains and enjoyed games of catch with their party favors—tennis balls monogrammed "Lola."

TUNES

The party's DJs admitted that this was their first dog-party gig, but they were happy to oblige the all dog-themed song list, including such hits as "Who Let the Dogs Out" and Elvis's "Hound Dog."

THE FASHIONABLE GUESTS

The attire advice on the invitations (which were appropriately addressed to the dogs themselves) was "your favorite leash," but this chic crowd went above and beyond the cue with enthusiasm. Lola wore a wreath of roses and ribbons made to match the color theme introduced by the party's invitation—white and hot pink with black polka dots. Lola's friend Delilah, a stylish English bulldog, donned a child-size Capezio pink-and-lavender tutu. Swarovski crystal collars and LaCoste-style dog shirts were everywhere you looked, along with more fur and feather accessories than in a Neiman Marcus catalog.

Some attendees created their own one-of-a-kind pieces for the occasion. Jewelry designer Bonnie Basham brought her miniature longhaired dachshund Gypsy in a black shirt that read "Loca." "Actually, I bought that tube top for myself, but it was a little small," Basham revealed. "I realized it looked better on her than me, so I cut leg holes in it."

Amused by the fashionable crowd were actress Janine Turner and daughter Juliette, whose toy poodle Cream Puff wore a leopard collar and leash and with red bows.

pet party cakes

Teri Aguilar of Ruff Life advises her clients "to treat dog party attendees just like you would children at a birthday party." Even though her made-to-order pet cakes are all natural with no added sugar, salt or preservatives, she recommends not letting a dog eat the entire cake at one sitting. Ruff Life offers two flavors of cakes, banana carob chip and applesauce spice, which are customized for the occasion with cream cheese frosting. www.ruff-life.org

Francesca Castagnoli, author of *Princess, You Know Who You Are*, attended with her dog Chewie, a bichon friese named after Princess Leia's friend Chewbacca in *Star Wars*. Chewie, who for this occasion was dressed in rhinestone collar and ribbon leash, has been known to cause such a frenzy on walks in Manhattan that Castagnoli says she can almost empathize with paparazzi-stalked stars.

LET THEM EAT CAKE

Of course, no birthday party is complete without birthday cake, and Lola's customized applesauce spice doggie birthday cake, baked by Teri Aguilar of online dog specialty store Ruff Life, was a huge hit among the guests. Lola blew out her bone-shaped candles, no doubt wishing for another year full of doggie soirees.

howl-oween party

WINSTON THE BEAGLE, SANDIE THE GOLDEN RETRIEVER, LULU THE YORKSHIRE TERRIER, AND SNOOP THE TOY POODLE HAVE A FAVORITE HOLIDAY—HALLOWEEN.

Their family's home has become famous for its yearly spooky displays, including a replica graveyard and circles of tall ghosts that blow in the wind. Although the scene might seem scary at night, during the day it makes for a perfect playground for this family of dogs. So the foursome decided, since this festive venue was literally in their own front yard, why not invite their friends over for some "Howl-oween" fun?

COSTUME CALL

The enticing invitation designed by Alyssa Reeves of Paradise Design Co.—packaged and mailed in a bone-shaped treat tin—specified costumes, and these guests dressed to impress. Some came as insects: Marley the Papillion/Poodle mix as a bumblebee, and Lilly and Indie, the Jack Russell Terriers, a butterfly and a ladybug. Some channeled other animals: Lola the Chihuahua decided she'd be a bunny for the day, while Minnie the standard poodle made a fabulous frog and Luke was cleverly disguised as an alligator.

Hosts LuLu and Snoop showed up as superheroes Wonder Woman and "Super Dog," and their friend Skyler the Pomeranian looked doggone good as Pocahontas. The traditionalists were represented by Jake the beagle as a witch, Buster the beagle and Teresa the Maltese as pumpkins, and Sandie masquerading as a devil. And then there was Winston, who hammed it up as a hotdog.

THE DOGGIE BUFFET

The food spread for the dogs was "to beg for." Sweets resembling peanut butter cups were guarded by a giant spider. "Pupsicles" were shaped as ghosts, pumpkins and bats, and dog cookies were cutouts of cobwebs and black cats. Water was served in a pumpkin bowl. So as not to overindulge the guests with too many sweets, there were also orange stuffed chew toys served in a witch's black stew pot.

FROLIC AND FUN

The decked-out dogs sniffed each other and sniffed for
bones (rawhide ones, that is) in the graveyard. Sandie then
led the group in her favorite activity—bobbing for tennis
balls—while smaller and more fashion-oriented dogs
played dress-up with the extra costumes kept on hand by
the hosts in case of any wardrobe malfunctions.

PERSONALIZED PUMPKIN CARVING

While the dogs paraded around the
party, Benjamin Vincent from Encore
Productions Entertainment sketched
each one and then carved the dog's
likeness into a real pumpkin, which
became a personalized party favor.

fido
framed

ART-LOVING LABRADORS ABBY AND MEGAN ARE USED TO CHIC ART GALLERY PARTIES HOSTED BY THEIR OWNERS, SINGER GEORGE MICHAEL AND GOSS GALLERY OWNER KENNY GOSS.

So the cultured canines decided to host their own gallery party for dogs, themed "Fido Framed" and featuring—what else—portraits of man's best friend. When the guests arrived for cocktails and kibble, they found a scene strikingly similar to an art gallery party for humans, but with brilliant dog-themed details that delighted the guests of honor and their owners.

The main attraction, of course, was dog portraits in varying media by artists from across the country. The portraits were displayed throughout the gallery at dog's-eye level so the dogs could better enjoy the works and no doubt contemplate which artist they should commission to paint their own portraits.

ART IMITATES LIFE

A professional photographer captured the look of each pooch as it posed upon its red carpet–like arrival. During the party, the photographs were inserted into a Paw Prints photo album, which was given to the dog's owner as a party favor.

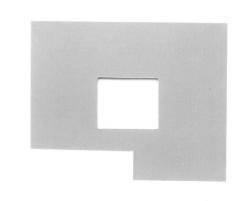

fido:framed

PORTRAITS OF MAN'S BEST FRIEND

You & your four-legged companion
are invited to join
Kenny Goss, George Michael
and their dogs Abby and Megan
for cocktails & kibble

21 March 2005
7 to 10
Goss Gallery

2500 CEDAR SPRINGS DALLAS, TEXAS 75201

CAROB, CHAMPAGNE AND CAVIAR TREATS

Since gallery parties are often elegant affairs, so was the dog party fare. Real chocolate is a no-no for dogs, so Sherrie Di Felice of Blind Dog Catering provided a carob fountain. A variety of brown and green dog treats (to match the party's decor) were available for delicious dipping. The fountain was the hit of the party, with the dogs begging for seconds and thirds and trying to dip their own treats when their owners weren't looking.

CHOCOLATE VS. CAROB

It's true that chocolate is bad for dogs. Chocolate contains caffeine and theobromine, which stimulate a dog's nervous system and can cause restlessness, hyperactivity, muscle twitching, increased urination, and excessive panting. The high fat content can also lead to upset stomach and vomiting. As a result, it should never be given to dogs. (See more on chocolate in Veterinarian Mandy Waller's tips for dog parties, page 95.) When catering dog parties, Sherrie Di Felice of Blind Dog Catering uses carob instead, which is caffeine- and theobromine-free. Di Felice explains that carob is "100 percent safe for your dog, and they love the taste." Her carob-flavored creations and carob dipping fountains are perfect treats for your furry companions. Bone appétit!

The doggie cuisine also included what looked like gourmet chocolates but were actually carob and yogurt confections; some were even labeled "Dogiva." Others were the shape of an artist's palette. "They taste like mints to dogs," Di Felice explains, "and are safe for them to eat." The dog cookies—which were shaped as champagne bottles and caviar containers, complete with brand names such as Osetra and Beluga— were passed on serving pieces that were real artists' palettes purchased from an art supply store. Even the stuffed dog toys were chocolate-covered strawberries and champagne bottles titled "Dog Perignon." Nothing but the finest for these discerning dogs.

And the people food was just as canine chic. The dog owners enjoyed beverages served in bone-shaped bottles and cookies that pictured art masterpieces such as the Mona Lisa inset with images of dogs.

CANINE COUTURE

Just as you would expect at a gallery event, the dogs came dressed to kill. It was an uptown/downtown mix of stylish characters, some in biker couture and others, such as Jackie, a standard poodle, wearing what looked like Chanel. CoCo, a Pomeranian, stole the show as she mixed and mingled in a leather jacket, boots and oversized sunglasses. "CoCo adores parties," said Janet Rosell Rice, her owner.

DOG PORTRAITS PROVIDED BY

- Anne Watkins—Watercolors..........www.annewatkins.com
- ArtPaw—Digital Prints..................www.artpaw.com
- Carol Pace—Acrylic on canvas.....www.mycolorsite.com
- Deborah O'Connor—Silhouettes...www.silhouetteartist.net
- Deborah Samuel—Photographs...http://www.deborahsamuel.com
- Rita Shugart—Oil on canvas........www.artbyrita.com
- Melanie Peskett —Oil on canvas

THEIR OWN WORK OF ART

Before Megan and Abby's friends departed, they each contributed to a one-of-a-kind "guest book" that consisted of several canvases. The dogs painted their own paw prints on the canvases, with paint and brushes reflecting the party's color scheme, each leaving behind their own creatively inspired mark.

a dog "I do"

FOR BETTER OR FOR WORSE, HUMANS CAN'T SEEM TO GET ENOUGH OF WEDDINGS. SO WHEN THERE IS A LULL IN THE WEDDING SEASON, WHY NOT CELEBRATE LOVE WITH A CANINE WEDDING? TYING THE KNOT HAS NEVER BEEN SO MUCH FUN.

THE WEDDING PARTY

This pooch party was the marriage of Princess the Chihuahua and Sweet Baboo the Tibetan terrier, who were obedience school sweethearts. Nancy Hathorn Sheets, owner of Tails of the City dog boutique, served as wedding planner, couturier, and event designer.

Since many dog lovers want their four-legged companions to be part of their own wedding festivities, Hathorn Sheets is often called upon to create floral wreath neckwear or custom outfits so the dogs have their own special attire for their owner's big day. If it is the dogs themselves that are getting hitched, custom clothing for the entire canine wedding party is in order.

THE CEREMONY

At the altar, a wedding-themed fabric dog bed was positioned for the bride and groom, with matching dog beds on either side for the wedding party. Princess's ring was a diamond-ring chew toy. Due to short attention spans, the ceremony was short. And even for these well-behaved dogs, posing patiently for wedding portraits proved to be a challenge. For these nuptials, Princess wore a Chihuahua-sized bridal dress and Sweet Baboo was fitted out in a tuxedo and top hat.

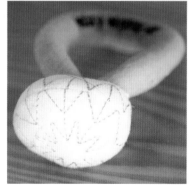

The bridesmaids (including Lola Chihuahua, Roxy the Bedlington Terrier, and Doodles, a Tibetan Terrier) wore elegant matching dresses, while the groomsmen (Beagles Jake and Buster along with McCoy, a Tibetan Terrier) looked dapper in coordinated vests and suits. Family members were given personalized decorative corsages for their collars, which stated their specific relation to the bride and groom: mother of the bride, father of the groom, etc. All of the dogs seemed pleased with their outfits—especially the bridesmaids, who might even wear their dresses again!

Breed-specific dog topiaries decorated the garden where the reception was held. The dogs were served individual doggie wedding cakes on color-coordinated china set on a doggie table covered in rose petals. Nearby, the people guests enjoyed a dog-themed cake, which are also commonly used at people weddings as a tribute by the bride and groom to their pets. This cake was topped with black and white vintage kissing Poodle figurines. Water, tea, and other beverages were served from different dog breed pitchers.

At the reception the four-legged guests played with chew toys shaped like champagne bottles and the distinctive blue gift boxes of Tiffany's packaging. After female white Labrador Hampton May caught the chew toy bouquet (and then played keep away with it), the delighted guests hoped that she and her live-in Labrador, Genghis, "would be next" so they could all attend another doggie wedding soon.

world by the tail

WITH THE EXPERTISE OF EVENT PLANNER/DESIGNER RAYMOND KELLY OF CHATEAU FLEUR, ANOTHER PARTY IDEA WAS BORN. THIS WAS A CELEBRATION OF THE DIFFERENT HERITAGE AND NATIVE LANGUAGES OF LOLA THE CHIHUAHUA AND HER DIVERSE BREEDS OF FRIENDS.

The plan was for the dogs and their owners to learn about the different breeds' heritage, sample their cuisine, enjoy patriotic decorations, and teach the dogs some commands in their native tongues.

THE INSPIRATION

Kelly created the party's country-themed decor and accessories to match. "Dog lovers see dogs as different types of people based not only on their personality and size, but also their heritage," said Kelly. "When hosting any type of party, the more comfortable you make the guests feel, the more successful the party is." So in this case, a place setting, cake, and treats were specifically designed as tributes to each dog breed's country of origin. Lola, for instance, was about to sit down to a fiesta.

MEXICO

The Mexican-themed place setting included red pepper- and sombrero-shaped dog treats, a dog piñata filled with dog cookies, and a cake iced with the flag of Mexico. Lola dressed for the occasion in a fantastic pink poncho and sombrero. After learning some commands in espagñol, she decided that, in keeping with her heritage, it was time for an afternoon siesta.

ITALY

It was amoré at first bite when Luigi the Italian Greyhound was treated to "puppy ciao," parmigian twists, puppy pizza, and biscotti cookies. Of course, he wore nothing less than a collar and leash of the finest Italian leather and barked about the latest soccer match with his friends from England and Spain.

EAST ASIA

Pumpkin the Pekinese feasted on "poochi sushi" and treats featuring Chinese symbols and dragons. The Asian-inspired place setting was complete with chopsticks and a "doggie bag" in the form of a wonton to-go box. Within the hour she was ready to eat again.

FRANCE

Jacqueline the French Poodle, who greeted her friends with a double lick on arrival, was delighted with the "ooh la la" French china and "bone jour" placemat in her honor. She was served Eiffel Tower and *je t'aime* themed dog treats as she lounged on a trés chic Eiffel Tower blanket with matching stuffed bone. Jacqueline simply had to dress in a jacket inspired by the designs of the most famous Parisian designer, Coco Chanel.

ENGLAND

It was only proper that Rocky Arnott the English Bulldog had tea and crumpets. Cigar-shaped treats and accessories recalled the time of Winston Churchill. To pay homage to the royal family, the "bulldog" bones were served in a dog bowl of crown jewels fit for a king.

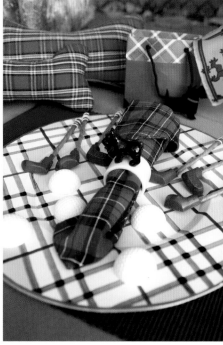

SCOTLAND

Baby the Scotty arrived wearing a canine kilt in honor of her heritage. Her assigned seat was a vision of plaid. Treats included "golf club" rawhide bones, yogurt "golf balls," and plaid chew toys.

U.S.A.

And finally, Mr. Magoo the American mutt felt right at home with the "burger and fries" treats in a fast food basket complete with mustard and ketchup. Doggie doughnuts were served on red, white, and blue plates. True to his roots, our all-American guy spent most of the party enjoying his baseball chew toy.

LANGUAGE COMMANDS

ITALIAN

come here = *vieni qua*

sit = *seduto*

bring it here = *portolo*

cookie = *biscotto*

speak = *parla*

FRENCH

here = *ici*

sit = *assis*

fetch = *cherches*

cookie = *le biscuit*

stay= *restes*

JAPANESE

fetch = *tottekoi*

cookie = *kukki*

come = *koi*

down = *fuse*

sit= *osuwari*

SPANISH

fetch = *agárralo*

come = *ven*

sit = *siéntate*

stay = *no te muevas*

shake hands = *dame la mano*

GERMAN

come = *komm*

sit = *sitz*

stay = *bleib*

kiss = *kuss*

good dog = *guter hund*

slumber party

WHEN IT'S TIME FOR AN OUT-OF-TOWN TRIP WITHOUT MAN'S BEST FRIEND, IT'S HARD TO SAY WHO HAS MORE SEPARATION ANXIETY—THE DOG OWNER OR THE DOG ITSELF.

So what better way to comfort a dogsick owner and cheer up a dog with the blues than to host a slumber party for the dog while the owner is away. For Lola's slumber party, her friends gathered at Kimberly's K-9 Fitness Center & Spa for a night of movies and more.

ATTIRE

The invitation instructed pooches to bring their own pajamas. Jack the Miniature Pincher arrived in what looked like a traditional men's set, while Uno the Chihuahua donned pink flannel rubber ducky pajamas. Lola wore pink cat-and-heart PJs that were custom made to match a pair of her owner's.

SLEEPING QUARTERS

The familiar faces of her friends comforted Lola, as did her own pink feather bed, brought to the spa from her home for the party. Her friends enjoyed matching beds provided by linen specialty store Porthault. Although each dog had its own plush bed, many decided that snuggling together was more fun.

SNACKS

The doggie snacks were made to model the food normally found at a child's slumber party—candy and junk food. Although these dog treats were made from healthy all-natural ingredients, they were disguised as candy brands such as Milky Woof and Mr. GoodDog. Peanut butter treats called "pupcakes" were a hit, alongside rawhide bones decorated with sprinkles. Dog cookies in the shape of ice cream cones made the perfect substitute for the make-your-own-sundae-bar treats popular at slumber parties.

ACTIVITIES

In addition to the dog-themed movie marathon, the guests exercised on dog-designed treadmills and played in the spa/hotel facilities. Some chose to indulge in grooming delights such as manicures, massages, and spa baths. When the other dogs wanted to stay up later than Lola, she got her beauty sleep with the help of her very own sleeping mask. She slept soundly knowing she was in good company while her parents were away.

RECOMMENDED MOVIES:

101 Dalmatians
Lady and the Tramp
Lassie
All Dogs Go to Heaven
Benji
Turner and Hooch
Best In Show

christmas/ chew-anuka party

DON'T FORGET YOUR PETS DURING THE HOLIDAY PARTY SEASON! FOR THIS PARTY, LOLA CHIHUAHUA AND HER FRIENDS WERE TREATED TO A HOWL-IDAY BASH CELEBRATING BOTH CHRISTMAS AND CHANUKAH.

Decking the Halls

The doggie decor for this event included cozy dog beds for lounging that read "Merry Christmas to all and to all a good night." Accompanying pillows were stitched to say, "Dear Santa, I've been a good dog." Decorative lights were draped on doghouses, and Christmas stockings featuring each dog breed were hung on the mantel. Plenty of other holiday decorations set the scene, but there were no poinsettia plants, as those can be toxic to dogs if ingested.

Dressed for the Season

Dogs came dressed in their festive holiday finest. Chic Chihuahuas Sable and Coco arrived in stylish mink and sable fur coats. Sweetie the Yorkie 'tis'ed the season in her Santa hat. Coco the Yorkie made her tribute by wearing a festive garland collar. Buster and Buddy the Springer Spaniels jingled all the way in their holiday collars of ribbons and bells.

Pet Portraits with Santa

With the dogs enthusiastically displaying their holiday spirit, it was the perfect opportunity to have their portraits made with Santa. The owners could then order Christmas or Chanukah cards featuring their dog's holiday photo. Customized phrases for the cards included dog-inspired sentiments such as "May you 'paws' to remember the spirit of the holidays" and "Have a paws-itively fabulous holiday season!"

Festive Fare

At this dog party, even the gingerbread house was a doghouse. The pooches also enjoyed cookies and molds in both Christmas and Chanukah themes. Humans were served their own holiday fare, including the popular seasonal drink "egg-dog."

Holiday Trees

Dogs get excited about holiday trees, and in case one should get knocked over, two trees were decorated for this affair. One sparkled with all dog-bone-shaped ornaments. The other was decorated with dog toys, and each dog chose a toy as a party favor. Since these dogs had all been nice and only occasionally naughty, they also received gifts from the party's Santa wrapped with ribbon that read "Santa Claws."

Tail alert!
Remember that when bigger dogs are near holiday trees, there's a good chance ornaments will end up in flight. Place the delicate ornaments higher up, out of tail's way.

puppy shower

IF ANY DOG WAS IN NEED OF A PARTY, IT WAS LOLA THE GREAT DANE, WHO WAS EXPECTING TEN TO TWELVE LITTLE DANES. SO PASHA, A TOY POODLE, INVITED A FEW OF LOLA'S FANCY FRIENDS TO THEIR HOME FOR AN ELEGANT PUPPY SHOWER IN LOLA'S HONOR.

THE DOGGIE TABLE

Lola's owner and the party's co-hostess, interior designer Michelle Nussbaumer, created gorgeous blue-and-white tablescapes for both the dogs and their doting owners. The doggie table was low to the ground, an appropriate "dog-level" for most of the guests, although some, like Lola the Great Dane, towered over it while the smaller set, like Lola the Chihuahua, sat on the table to sip and socialize. The table was set with porcelain dog bowls, chargers, and bone-shaped chew toys substituted for silverware and arranged accordingly. The seating arrangements were comfy for all—custom-made blue and white pillows for the dogs and garden seats of the same colors for the owners.

The owners also had their own party table nearby, with plenty of chilled champagne and other people-only delights that their four-legged friends couldn't reach (except maybe Lola, but her pregnancy made her too tired to interfere).

The hostess passed around a silver tray filled with dog treats and toys, letting dogs choose their own. Most dogs obeyed the one-treat-at-a-time rule; the rawhide bones were declared the favorite, and the squeaky pacifier toys ran a close second.

PUPPY CHOW

The main course consisted of a "puppy chow" with a touch of gravy to keep tails wagging. Dessert was yogurt treats and dog biscuits, all baby-themed in pastel pink or blue.

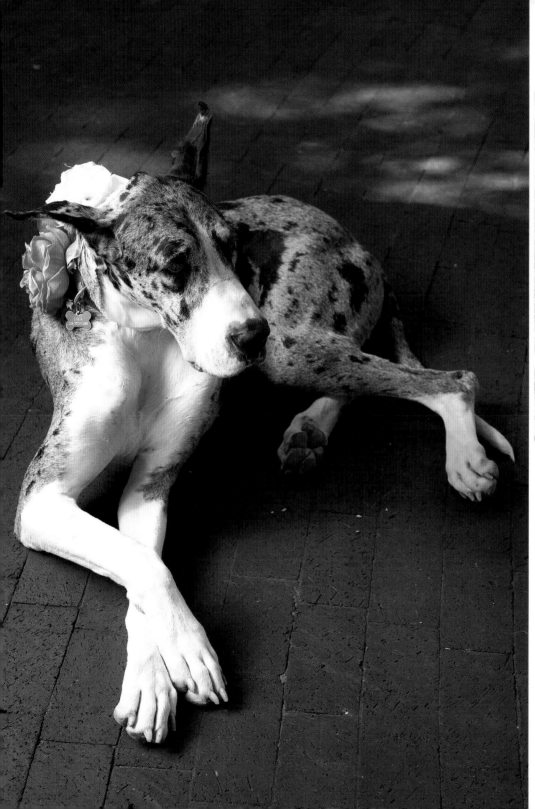

BABY "BOOTIE"

Lola had registered at a nearby pet boutique, and the guests came bearing gifts. Some of the dogs got involved in the unwrapping, but when the paper, ribbon, and multitude of bows were cleared, there were enough puppy blankets, stuffed animals, and rattles for the entire litter. Lola also loved the pillows and bags featuring pooch portraits of herself and her friends.

PUPPY LOVE

For the most part, the dogs displayed impeccable table manners. The Poodles Coco Bella and Pasha compared bows and beauty secrets. Corkscrew the Dachshund was a bit shy and stayed close to her owner. Marilyn the Corgie and Isabell the British Bull Terrier had to be separated briefly after a tiff—perhaps they were arguing over puppy names. But Big Lola and little Lola demonstrated that even opposites can be best friends, and a puppy shower is no place for cat fights.

We grow, we learn, and we heel
but for now, we paws to celebrate

WE, THE CLASS OF
TWO THOUSAND AND FIVE
OF PUPPY HIGH SCHOOL
PROUDLY ANNOUNCE
OUR COMMENCEMENT EXERCISES
ON THE TWENTY-FIRST OF MAY
AT NOON
THE DOG PARK AT CEDAR BEND

Theresa Clossey

13200 HILLSIDE DRIVE
DALLAS, TEXAS 75225

why don't you…

DIPLOMA

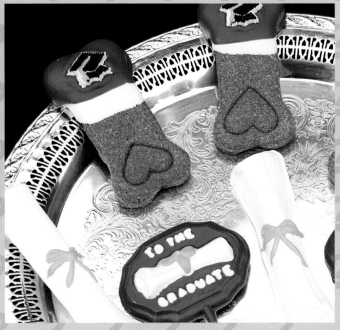

. . . CELEBRATE YOUR DOG'S GRADUATION FROM OBEDIENCE SCHOOL, complete with doggie graduation cap and gown and diploma, as Jeanne Marie Clossey did for her Maltese, Theresa.

. . . THROW A WATER PARTY FOR YOUR DOG.

Whether it's a lawn sprinkler, a pond, or an entire beach, most dogs love a frolic in the water (preferably with Frisbees and balls). Just keep an eye on them, especially in the surf.

. . . **HOST A "BARK" MITZVAH** as actress Amy Davidson did for her Yorkie, Stanley. "I never had my own bas mitzvah, so I decided to host one for my dog Stanley instead," she explains. It was a great excuse to get all of Stanley's friends together and spoil them with attention and treats. Stanley wore the traditional yarmulke for the celebration.

. . . **DRESS THE PART YOURSELF** with fun dog-themed clothing and accessories.

. . . PLAN A FUNDRAISER FOR YOUR FAVORITE ANIMAL-FRIENDLY CHARITY, like this "Posh Dog Fashion Show" (right). With or without theme costumes, the runway show is sure to generate warm applause and plenty of pats on the head.

. . . *HOST A "TAME YOUR WILD ANIMAL" PARTY.* Create a wild animal theme with animal-print decor and chew toys. Invite a dog trainer to teach a class at the party. Instead of dreading obedience training, this will make it fun for both dogs and owners. . .

. . . **THROW A DOGGIE VALENTINE'S PARTY** such as Joe Perry's "Won't You Be My Basset-tine" party for her Basset Hound, Bogie.

. . . **GIVE BACK TO THE COMMUNITY** by volunteering your dog and yourself for animal-assisted therapy at a hospital or nursing home. These Labs are volunteers along with their owner at Baylor Hospital in Dallas.

veterinarian's party tips

- Make sure your dog has had all of its shots, including the kennel cough vaccine.

- Ideally, all dog party attendees should be spayed or neutered (this is generally done by six months of age). All intact male and female dogs should be kept separate or there will be more fun at the party than expected!

- Dogs that are sick (such as coughing or having nasal discharge) should send their regrets and stay at home.

- If children are involved, make sure they know how to approach dogs carefully. Even kid-friendly dogs might be nervous in an unfamiliar environment.

- If you are hosting an indoor party, keep all other house pets (cats, rabbits, hamsters, birds, etc.) out of harm's way. Even the best-trained dogs are susceptible to "pack" behavior in a moment of high excitement.

- Keep the party area clean, and pick up after the guests to avoid spreading germs.

- Keep extra leashes on hand in case some guests forget to bring theirs.

- Do not serve meat (such as chicken) containing bones that can cause choking.

- Avoid giving the dogs fatty foods, as grease can cause everything from upset stomachs to pancreatitis.

- Avoid giving dogs even small amounts of chocolate.

- Keep dogs away from poinsettias and oleander plants.

- Dogs should not eat before running, swimming, etc. Exercising on a full stomach can cause nausea and vomiting.

- Be sure to provide plenty of fresh, cool water for all.

- Have the local animal clinic phone number and address handy in case of emergency.

thank-yous

This book was a blast to put together, and Lola and I owe a great deal of thanks and big wet puppy dog kisses to a great group of people:

Teri Aguilar and Ruff Life, Amy Alford and Buster and Buddy, Amanda and Blake Andrews and Luke, Dina and Jason Arnott and Rocky, Francesca Castagnoli and Chewey, Jeanne Marie Clossey and Theresa, Rebecca Collins and Art Paw, Amy Davidson and Stanley, Sherrie and Frank Di Felice and Mr. Magoo, Anne and Kirk Douglas and The Dog Bible, Emily Eagle, Encore Productions and Entertainment and Benjamin Vincent, George Michael, Kenny Goss and Megan and Abby, Caroline True, Alycen Cuellar, Natalie Quintanilla, Jessica Olsson, James Cope and the Goss Gallery, Green Piece Wire Art, Kimberly Hamilton and Kimberly's K-9 Fitness and Spa, Allison Hopkins and Skylar, Dale Horst, Marisa Newkirk Huckin, Kristen Karlisch, Raymond Kelly, Margo and Jim Keyes and Opus, Le Gateau, Betty Lidgi and Coco and Sable, Cheryl and Alex Lilley, Cheryl Luster, Jan Miller Rich and Schumacker and Genny, Pamela and Jarl Mohn, Sandra Mueller and Titi, Neiman Marcus, Blaine Nelson and Coco, Michelle Nussbaumer and Lola and Pasha, Deborah O'Connor, Carol Pace, Melanie Peskett, Betty Lou Phillips and Jackson, Porthault, Alyssa Reeves and Paradise Design Co., Farris Rookstool III, Janet Rosell Rice and Coco, Deborah Samuel, Ann Sappington and Baby, Nancy Hawthorne Sheets and Roxanne, Doodles and Sweet Baboo, Jan and Jim Showers and Sweetie, Gibbs Smith and Sophie, Susan Spindler and Jake and Buster, Sheri Staten and Pumpkin, Summerlee Staten and Beaufort, Laurel Thomaschaske, Tolleson Family with Winston, Sandy, LuLu and Snoop, Amy Tolleson, Stephanie Vandegrift, Marty Walker, Dr. Mandy Waller and the team at Park Cities Animal Hospital, Anne Watkins, White Oaks Ranch.

Gladys Gonzalez, John Carrabino, Annie Jeeves, Jan Planit, and Gary Sommerstein—I am so grateful for your hard work, support, friendship and belief in me.

Thank you to all of the very talented photographers who contributed to the book—Stephen Karlisch, Lorenzo Hodges, Justin Whitman, James Dimmock, Jeff Sinelli, Paul Skipworth, Danny Piassick, and Michael Jenkins.

Courtney Dreslin and Hampton and Ghengis—I am so lucky to have such a great writing partner. Thank you for your hard work and friendship.

Madge, thank you for being such an enthusiastic editor for the second time! I look forward to many more projects together.

Caroline—Big kiss and thank you for your contributions to this project.

I feel so lucky to be a part of the Whitman Family now! Beth and Kipp Whitman and Madison, thank you for blessing our family with Minnie!

To my incredible family, Big Mama, Daddy, Kirby, Kari, and Krystal, I love you so much, and I truly appreciate all of your support and help. Thank you for raising me to love animals.

Justin, I love you and I love the way you love Lola. Thank you for being such a supportive husband!